Presented to:

Sylvia Lambright

By:

Faith Axman

On the Occasion of:

year end Happy Day Club

Date:

3- 23 - 10

THE WAY OF
EXCELLENCE
LOVE

THE WAY OF
*E*XCELLENCE

LOVE

RAY PRITCHARD

MOODY PRESS
CHICAGO

Editorial Services: Julie-Allyson Ieron, Joy Media

Design: Ragont Design

ISBN: 0-8024-3179-8

1 3 5 7 9 10 8 6 4 2

Printed in the United States of America

For Nick

He makes the world smile.

*"A happy heart
makes the
face cheerful."*
PROVERBS 15:13

CONTENTS

LOVE OF A LIFETIME   12

BLESSED PEACEMAKERS   16

SPEAKING THE TRUTH IN LOVE   26

UNITY IN THE GOSPEL   36

FROM THE SAME WOMB   46

TOUGH LOVE   56

CHRISTIAN LIBERTY   66

IS THERE A SERVANT IN THE HOUSE?   76

MERCY PEOPLE   86

MORE THAN CONQUERORS   96

NOTHING CAN SEPARATE US   106

LOVE THAT LASTS FOREVER   116

Love of a Lifetime

I know two things for certain about love:

Love is a choice, not a feeling.
Love is a gift—from God to us and from us to
others.

We love because we choose to love, not because we feel like loving. Sometimes love
reaches out, and sometimes love lets go. Corrie

ten Boom told of Christian friends who wronged her in a public and malicious way. For many days she was bitter and angry until she forgave them. But in the night she would wake up thinking about what they had done, and she would get angry all over again. The memory would not go away.

Help came from her Lutheran pastor to whom she confessed her frustration after two sleepless weeks. "Corrie, up in the church tower is a bell that is rung by pulling on a rope. When the sexton pulls the rope, the bells peals out ding-dong, ding-dong, ding-dong. But when he stops pulling on the rope, the sound slowly fades away. Forgiveness is like that. When we forgive someone, we take our hand off the rope. But if we've been tugging at our grievances for a long time, we mustn't be surprised if the old angry thoughts keep coming for a while. They are just the ding-dongs of the old bell slowing down."

That pastor is right. Sooner or later we all have to let go of the rope of anger and bitterness. It's like that with love. Love chooses. Love acts. Love moves into a hard situation. Love gives when it knows the gift will not be understood or appreciated. And sometimes, as Corrie ten Boom learned, love chooses to let go.

The most famous verse in the Bible tells us God so loved the world that He gave His one and only Son for us. Love is a choice and a gift that starts with God, comes down to us, and then flows out to others. First God, then us, then others. You might call this the

Greater Golden Rule: We do unto others as God has
done unto us.

❧

In the next few pages we're going to look at love
from many perspectives. We'll talk about peacemakers, truth tellers, tough lovers, and free people who for
love's sake give up their liberty. We'll look at servants
and mercy people who bring God's sunshine into this
dark world. The book ends with a focus on the love of
God in Christ that never lets go of us no matter how
desperate our circumstances.

❧

Love must be shared, or it withers and dies. Love is a
choice and gift. Don't keep it to yourself. Give it away.

"They truly love who show their love" Shakespeare

Blessed
Peacemakers

Matthew 5:9

"*Blessed are the
peacemakers, for they will
be called sons of God.*"

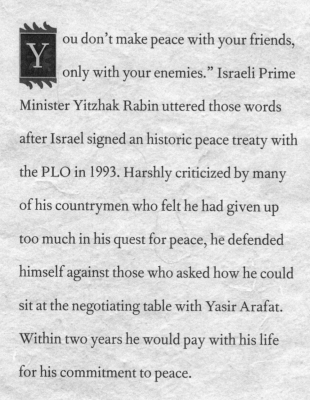

ou don't make peace with your friends, only with your enemies." Israeli Prime Minister Yitzhak Rabin uttered those words after Israel signed an historic peace treaty with the PLO in 1993. Harshly criticized by many of his countrymen who felt he had given up too much in his quest for peace, he defended himself against those who asked how he could sit at the negotiating table with Yasir Arafat. Within two years he would pay with his life for his commitment to peace.

Whatever else we may say about Mr. Rabin, we must acknowledge the truth of his words. Peacemaking is a risky, difficult business. It's easier to start a war than to end one.

According to an article in *Today in the Word*, a group of academics and historians has noted that, "Since 3600 B.C., the world has known only 292 years of peace. During this period there have been 14,351 wars, large and small, in which 3.64 billion people have been killed. The value of the property destroyed is equal to a golden belt around the world 97.2 miles wide and thirty-three feet thick. Since 650 B.C., there have also been 1656 arms races, only sixteen of which have not ended in war. The remainder ended in the economic collapse of the countries involved." [1]

John Foster Dulles pinpoints the problem in these words: "The world will never have lasting peace so long as men reserve for war the finest human qualities. Peace, no less than war, requires idealism and self-sacrifice, and a righteous and dynamic faith."

❧

Dulles is right. Peace never just happens. You have to go out of your way to make peace. That is why Jesus said, "Blessed are the peace*makers*"—not the peace-wishers nor the peace-hopers. In a world torn

❧

Jesus said, "Love your enemies and pray for those who persecute you" (Matthew 5:44). First He said it, then He showed us how to do it when He died on the cross.

❧

by strife and fueled by hatred, we need Christians who will step into the breach as true peacemakers.

Peacemaking takes courage, because you never know how the other person is going to respond. If you make that phone call, or go see your boss, or write a letter to your mother, that other person might not understand, take it as a sign of weakness, try to twist your motives. But if you have a broken relationship and you do nothing, things will get worse.

Proverbs 24:26 says, "An honest answer is like a kiss on the lips." The truth may hurt, but it is more satisfying in the end.

Peacemaking requires patience—the willingness to wait for God to solve our problems. Many times we get frustrated with other people because they aren't changing fast enough to suit us. Parents get angry at their children, husbands at wives, wives at husbands, children at parents, workers at bosses, bosses at workers, students at teachers, friends at friends, relatives at relatives, church members at church members.

In the 1960s Dr. Martin Luther King Jr. asked his followers to sign the following pledge:

- Meditate daily on the teachings and life of Jesus. Remember always that the movement seeks justice and reconciliation—not victory.

- Walk and talk in the way of love, for God is love.

- Pray daily to be used by God so that all men might be free.

- Observe with both friend and foe the ordinary rules of courtesy.

- Seek to perform regular service for others and for the world.

- Refrain from the violence of fist, tongue, or heart.

Those principles strike me as wise. Think about the strained relationships in your life. Will you be the one to pick up the phone or write a letter? Will you stop making excuses and make the first move?

Jesus made the first move when He humbled Himself by leaving heaven to be born as a baby. He showed us what it means to take the initiative to heal a broken relationship.

Go with me to bloody Calvary. Gaze on the disfigured body of Jesus of Nazareth. Can you hear the howling mob? They scream for His blood; they cheer His pain; they laugh at His suffering. Chanting, jeering, mocking. The mob enjoys every moment of this tragedy. A man dies and the world cheers.

Yet from the cross come words that have echoed across the ages, "Father, forgive them, for they do not know what they are doing."

Now we know. If we never knew before, now we

know. We know the price; we know the pain; we know the agony. If you want to see the real face of love, look to the cross. If you want to see kindness, gaze on the contorted face of the crucified Redeemer.

Jesus said, "Love your enemies and pray for those who persecute you" (Matthew 5:44). First He said it, then He showed us how to do it when He died on the cross.

Would you like to make peace with your enemies? You can, but it won't be easy. If you would rather live in anger and bitterness, that option is always open.

Or you can follow Jesus to the cross and die there.

The choice is yours.

*Lord Jesus,
Make me an
instrument of Your
peace. Give me
the courage to get
involved when I
would rather walk
away. Amen*

*Name three peacemakers you have known. What qualities
did they have in common?*

What steps do you need to take to heal broken relationships?

*Reread the commitments Dr. Martin Luther King Jr. asked
his followers to make. Put your initials by those commitments if you are willing to follow them.*

Speaking the Truth in Love

Ephesians 4 : 15

Instead, speaking the truth in love,

we will in all things grow up into him

who is the Head, that is, Christ.

Jesus is the only person who ever perfectly balanced truth and love. John 1:14 tells us He was "full of grace and truth." What a wonderful phrase. He spoke the truth, and He radiated God's love. He loved sinners. He encouraged every genuine seeker who crossed His path. And He answered every question—the honest and the insincere. That same Jesus rebuked the Pharisees, cleared out the temple courtyard with a whip, and repeatedly spoke truth to the powerful elite without regard for His own safety.

Jesus was called a "friend of sinners." He loved the lost and felt at home with them. He hung out with drunkards and gluttons; fallen women felt comfortable in His presence. He welcomed proud Pharisees and curious soldiers. People in trouble and those with troubled hearts gravitated to Him. The only people He turned away were those who turned away from Him.

We face the same challenge today: to balance truth and love in all our relationships. We are to know the truth and to walk in love—all the time.

A friend said to me, "I don't know many lost people." He wasn't making an excuse but stating a fact.

Many of us have cut ourselves off from the lost all around us and for that reason have trouble sharing Christ with others. That's not anything to brag about. You can hardly win the lost if you don't know the lost. You can't reach a person with whom you have no contact. Jesus met Nicodemus at night and the woman at the well in broad daylight. He made them feel welcome to be with Him.

Sometimes Christians are afraid to share their faith because they feel inadequate to lead another person to Jesus Christ. What about those fears? My answer may surprise you. The reason you feel inadequate is because you *are* inadequate. Telling someone how to have their sins forgiven is an enormous responsibility. What if you foul it up, and they end up feeling worse? I suppose that would be like having a person ask you how to get to Atlanta, but you somehow get them so confused they end up in Amarillo instead.

Here's the bottom-line truth: You can't lead another person to Christ no matter what you do. You will never know all the answers to all the questions people ask. And you probably won't say all the right words.

❧

Jesus spoke the truth, and He radiated God's love. He loved sinners. He encouraged every genuine seeker who crossed His path. And He answered every question.

❧

Am I suggesting that Christians shouldn't do evangelism or that we should keep our religion private? Hardly. We are commanded by the Lord to go, preach the gospel, and make disciples. It's how we do it, or more accurately, how we think about it, that makes all the difference.

⚬

I spent a few minutes with a new Christian who, though raised in a church, had only recently trusted Christ as her Lord and Savior. Now she wants to help others, but she doesn't know where to begin. That's when I took out a piece of paper and wrote "God" on one side and "Your Friend" on the other. Then I drew circles representing links in a chain stretching from "Your Friend" to "God." I told her the good news about evangelism is: you don't have to lead a person to Christ. Only the Holy Spirit can do that. All you need to do—all you can do—is to be a link in the chain that God uses to bring people to Himself.

"I can do that," she said with a smile. We all can. Evangelism is the work of many people over time forming links in the chain that leads to heaven.

Build relationships. Take time to listen. Share what Christ has done for you. Let them know what Christ can do for them. And when you get the opportunity, invite them to join you as a fellow pilgrim walking by faith on the way of the cross.

Our part is to speak the truth in love. The rest is up to God.

❧

Lord Jesus Christ,

Give me the courage

to speak the truth and

the grace to speak it in

love. And if I can't

speak the truth in love,

help me not to speak

at all. Amen

❧

How does the life of Christ demonstrate a perfect balance between truth and love?

Which is worse—truth without love or love without truth?

How can you be a link in the chain of salvation for someone this week?

Unity in
the Gospel

I appeal to you, brothers, in the name of our Lord Jesus

Christ, that all of you agree with one another so that

there may be no divisions among you and that you may

be perfectly united in mind and thought.

he Bible has a great deal to say about the importance of unity among believers. Psalm 133:1 declares, "how good and pleasant it is when brothers live together in unity." In John 17:21 Jesus prayed, "that all of them may be one." We are instructed to "make every effort to keep the unity of the Spirit through the bond of peace" (Ephesians 4:3). And Romans 15:5 tells us the ultimate source of unity: "May the God who gives endurance and encouragement give you a spirit of unity."

Disagreement is okay, but disunity is a sin. Our goal should be unity—not uniformity. We will not all agree on secondary issues such as the proper mode of baptism, details of the Second Coming, church government, worship styles, Bible translations, and so on.

But some issues are nonnegotiable. This list includes the personal nature of God, the Trinity, the Bible as God's inspired Word, the Incarnation, the deity of

Jesus Christ as the Son of God—His Virgin Birth, His miracles, His death on the cross as an atonement for our sins, His bodily resurrection, His literal Second Coming to the earth, the personality of the Holy Spirit, salvation by grace alone through faith alone apart from human works, and the church as the bride of Christ. If a person comes to one of our churches and says, "Jesus is not the Son of God," we will put him out the front door—quickly!

The main question is this: How can Christians from different backgrounds live together in harmony? First, we must focus on the things that unite us—not the things that divide us. True Christians are united by a shared faith in Jesus Christ. Second, we must give fellow believers room to disagree on lesser issues. We don't have to look alike, talk alike, or pray in the same way, and we don't have to agree about spiritual gifts or how much water to use in baptism.

Don't feel like you need to convince everyone of the superiority of your own preferences.

Twentieth-century Christian philosopher Francis Schaeffer emphasized that our quest for unity must go beyond platitudes and reach the realm of observable love. Romans 15:2 reminds us that "each of us should please his neighbor for his good, to build him up." That means reaching out to those who see things differently. In some cases it means refusing to argue with them. In other cases it means meeting with them, praying with them, working with them, getting to know them. It means believers from different backgrounds should meet together for prayer, Bible study, worship, and evangelism. United action breaks down barriers that keep us apart.

Our goal is not outward agreement but love. In a fallen world, we'll never totally agree—and that's okay.

We don't need to have one denomination—or even just one church in every town. Different churches reflect different needs, backgrounds, and preferences. This is all to the good. But we must not let our differences outweigh God's call to love each other.

We are instructed to "make every effort to keep the unity of the Spirit through the bond of peace" (Ephesians 4:3). And Romans 15:5 tells us the ultimate source of unity: "May the God who gives endurance and encouragement give you a spirit of unity."

It is possible to disagree agreeably. This means stating your case calmly, kindly, honestly—and listening as the other person states his case. Sometimes it means agreeing to disagree—and moving on so you don't debate the same issues over and over. In all things we must let God be God. When we get to heaven, the Lord will sort things out for us once and for all. Until then we can baptize many different ways, sing in different styles, and put different labels on our churches.

Hold your convictions—but hold them in love. Robert Lightner tells of a practice used by Japanese parents when their children fight with one another. They bring each child into the room and put a square cushion on the table. One by one, each child puts his hands on the cushion and says, "I am right and my friend is wrong." He then moves to the other side, puts his hands on it, and says, "My friend is right and

I am wrong." The child then places his hands on the third side of the cushion, saying, "Both of us are right and both of us are wrong." As he places his hands on the final side, he says, "I am partly right and my friend is partly right."

When we get to heaven and look back on many of the issues that have divided us, we will say the same thing. *We were partly right, and our friends were partly right*. Between now and then, there are going to be plenty of disagreements in the church. That's the price we pay for being human.

Disagreements come with the territory—and they aren't always bad. Our diversity as Christians gives us a marvelous opportunity to demonstrate that Jesus Christ is the true center of our faith. May God grant us a true and deep Christian unity that transcends our earthly opinions.

Spirit of God,
Fill Your church with
such power that we will
be of one heart and one
mind. Cleanse me
from any divisive
spirit lurking in my
heart. Amen

List those Christian truths you would consider fundamental and nonnegotiable. What happens when any of these truths is compromised?

Why is Christian unity important to God? to the church? to the world?

When it comes to your relationship with other Christians, are you a uniter or a divider? What would your friends say?

From the Same Womb

1 T h e s s a l o n i a n s   4 : 9 – 1 0

Now about brotherly love we do not need to write to you,

for you yourselves have been taught by God to love each other.

And in fact, you do love all the brothers throughout Macedonia.

Yet we urge you, brothers, to do so more and more.

S ometimes we need to be reminded about things we already know. "Now about brotherly love we do not need to write to you." That's an interesting way to put it, isn't it? "I don't need to remind you about this, but I think I will anyway." The word for "brotherly love" in Greek is a word you already know. The Greek word is *philadelphia*. Outside the New Testament it is almost always used for love within a family. It comes from two Greek words joined together:

Philos means "tender affection, fondness, devotion." It implies an obligation to love.

Adelphos means "one born of the same womb."

So *philadelphia* means "tender affection owed to those born from the same womb." It's easy to understand why the early Christians adopted this word to describe Christian love. All Christians have been "born of the same womb" through new birth. Everyone who is saved is saved the same way. God doesn't have three different plans of salvation—Plan A for Protestants, Plan B for Catholics, and Plan C for everyone else. Jesus said, "You must be born again" (John 3:7). To be born again means to receive new life through personal faith in Jesus Christ. It means to be "born from God's womb."

I have three brothers—Andy, Alan, and Ron.

We're all different, and to prove it we live in four different states. We have different personalities, different habits and hobbies, different likes and dislikes. Yet one thing binds us together. We come from the same womb. There is a special place in my heart for my brothers, a bond between us that time and distance cannot break.

❧

The same truth applies in the spiritual realm. Everyone who belongs to Jesus belongs to me. I owe each of them tender affection and brotherly love.

❧

Note three facts about brotherly love: First, God teaches it. "For you yourselves have been taught by God to love each other." The word translated "taught by God" appears nowhere else in the New Testament. It speaks not of a lesson learned in a classroom but of truth learned through relationship. What's the best way to learn French? Live among people who speak French, who love French cuisine, and who appreciate French culture. The same is true regarding love. You learn to love by associating with loving people. Love isn't taught; it's caught. Because we come from the womb of God, we share His basic nature: love. Love ought to be the most natural thing for believers to express.

God's kingdom is not
limited to graduates of
one seminary or members
of one denomination or
to people who look, think,
and act just like we do.
God's kingdom embraces
all true believers.

Second, love reaches out to all God's children. "And in fact, you do love all the brothers throughout Macedonia." Underline the phrase—"all the brothers." Most of us love *some* of the brothers, maybe even *most* of the brothers. But *all* of them? We are to love all true believers, everywhere, all the time. No qualifications, no reservations. Most of us have inner qualifications. We don't like this group or that denomination. We're not comfortable with people who speak in tongues or use a prayer book. We may distrust people who have a different worship style.

❧

All such thinking is wrong. God's kingdom is not limited to graduates of one seminary or members of one denomination or to people who look, think, and act just like we do. God's kingdom embraces all true believers no matter what church they belong to, or even if they don't belong to any church. The love of God is not limited—not by nation or ocean or tribe or tongue or custom or clothing or race or politics or creed or caste or any other human condition. When the love of God captures us, our hearts will be as big as His.

This love should always be increasing in our lives. "Yet we urge you, brothers, to do so more and more." What does it mean that our love should increase? It means we should increase in our

- sympathy for those in need
- patience for those who are struggling
- tolerance toward those with whom we disagree

The most powerful recommendation for any church is that the members love one another. The world pines for this and flocks where it is found. What are the unchurched looking for in a church? Not a friendly church or a relevant church or a church with programs for kids. Not just a church where the Bible is taught. As essential as those are, they don't touch the deepest heart cry of this generation, which is for a place where they can be truly and deeply loved. When the people of the world find such a place, they stand in line to get in.

How does God help us grow in this area? By putting us in situations that force us to practice Christian love. Over the years I have observed God do this again and again. He allows two people to have difficulties with each other, often to the point of anger and bitterness. He does it because the only way we learn to love is by dealing with unlovely people. I have seen it happen between husbands and wives, parents and children, co-workers, neighbors, fellow students, and relatives. People who start out disliking each other often end up as dearest friends.

C. S. Lewis said, "We may talk so much about loving people in general that we love no one in particular." Yes, some people are so rude, inconsiderate, boorish, and unkind that it seems easier to walk away than to love them. Only the Holy Spirit can cause us to love the unlovely.

Yet, the church owes it to the Lord, each other, and the world to love as God loved us: So,

- let our hearts grow with brotherly love for all God's children;
- let Christian sympathy go out to those in need;
- let us pray for one another and especially for those with whom we disagree.

Heavenly Father,
You are a God of love,
and all true love comes
from You. Grant that we
might grow in love as we
grow in the knowledge
of You. Give us a heart
for the whole family
of God. Amen

In what ways are we taught to love by God?

In what area does your family need most to grow in love?

Think of three ways you can show love to a fellow Christian this week.

Tough
Love

1 Corinthians 5 : 1 2 – 1 3

What business is it of mine to judge those

outside the church? Are you not to judge

those inside? God will judge those outside.

"Expel the wicked man from among you."

A n incredible story stands behind these verses. A man in the church at Corinth had an affair with his father's wife. For some reason the church kept the man in the fellowship and did not discipline him for his egregious sin. How could Christians have harbored such a man? Perhaps they fell prey to the ancient heresy called antinomianism, which literally means "anti-law." This heresy teaches that once you come to Christ, it doesn't matter how you live. It suggests that since we are under grace and not under law, there are no binding rules for the Christian life.

Imagine the Corinthians saying, "We don't approve of what this man is doing, but we affirm that he is a brother in Christ." Such thinking leads to excusing sin instead of judging it. From there it is a short step to boasting about the sin you permit, because in some perverted way you think it magnifies the grace of God.

Eighteenth-century poet Alexander Pope penned these words of warning:

> *Vice is a monster of so frightful mien,*
> *As to be hated needs but to be seen;*
> *Yet seen too oft, familiar with her face,*
> *We first endure, then pity, then embrace.*

We've all heard the slogan, "friends don't let friends drive drunk." True Christian friends don't let other Christian friends off the hook when they sin. They say something; they do something. Paul is saying, "You should have done something about this man, but you didn't. I'm getting involved because you didn't. If you had done your job, I wouldn't have to do it for you."

Though it may not seem so at the time, discipline is an act of grace. When done for the right reason and in the right spirit, it is an act of kindness.

Writing in the *National Review* several years ago, Florence King commented that our declining response to hostility is the surest mark of our cultural decay. In the old days when faced with trouble we would say, "Let's take it outside." Now if someone offends us, we say, "Let's do lunch." We laud those who achieve bipartisan compromise. Where are the men and the women who, when faced with moral evil, will say, "Let's take it outside"?

That's what Paul is doing in 1 Corinthians 5. Paul is not timid. He proposes this man be cast from the church in a public meeting. He says when the church is gathered together, it should "hand this man over to Satan" (1 Corinthians 5:5). Remember Satan is the prince of this world who usurped the earth and made it his own after the Fall. Since then the world has been hostile to God and friendly to Satan. The world is his turf, but the church belongs to God. In that sense, a local church is like an outpost of heaven in enemy territory. To cast a person out of the church is to send him back into Satan's territory where he is cut off from the protection of the body of Christ.

The purpose is not just to purify the church; it is also to save the man's soul. Every promise Satan makes is eventually broken. Everyone who follows him ends up on the Boulevard of Broken Dreams. Paul hopes that by casting this man out into the world, he will suffer such pain and humiliation that in the end he will come to his senses.

Here is hope for parents of wayward children and spouses whose husbands or wives have left them. Sometimes you've got to be tough enough to open the door and let them leave. Some lessons can only be learned the hard way. Nothing tears at a parent or a spouse like seeing a loved one suffer. But how much worse it is if we stand in the way by paying the bills, bailing them out of jail, and providing a safety net so they won't hit rock bottom. Until our loved ones face the consequences of their sin, they will stay the way they are.

A few years ago our elders heard the story of a

man who had left his wife for another woman. As
we pondered what to do, one of the elders cau-
tioned against trying to repair the damage too
quickly. "If we try to get him off the hook, we may
interfere with God's plan to restore him." Sometimes God's judgment is His severe mercy to His
wayward children. Sometimes eager parents and
friends can block the work of God through being
soft when they ought to be hard, tender when they
ought to be tough.

I admit these are easy words to say and more difficult to apply. Though it may not seem so at the
time, discipline is an act of grace. When done for
the right reason and in the right spirit, it is an act of
kindness. Rarely will it be seen that way by the
person undergoing discipline or by the those who
must observe it. We can't pretend sin makes no difference. If we love our friends and if we believe in

God, sometimes the best thing we can do is to say, "Go your own way. I love you enough to let you go. When you are ready to come home, when you are tired of living in the far country, I'll be standing in the road waiting to welcome you home."

_Lord Jesus, You cared enough
to come for us while we were
living in sin. You died for us
while we were Your enemies.
Give us the tough love to let
go when we need to let go
and the faith to never give up
on those who have turned
away from You. Amen_

_Why do you think the church in Corinth harbored the man
living in open sin?_

In what way is discipline a sign of love?

_Is there a Christian friend you need to confront about his or
her sin? What do you plan to do about it?_

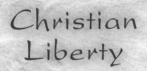

Christian Liberty

1 Corinthians 8:1

Now about food sacrificed to idols: We

know that we all possess knowledge.

Knowledge puffs up, but love builds up.

W hen was the last time you worried about whether or not you should eat meat offered to idols? Evidently that was a burning concern in the church at Corinth. While we may not understand all the details, Paul's point is clear: When some people saw meat that had been offered to idols, they couldn't get the idol off their minds. To them, eating that meat was an act of spiritual compromise. They ended up feeling unclean and sinful. For them, eating that meat was sinful even though it's not a sin in the eyes of God.

You can sin when you do something that God doesn't count as sinful. If you eat it and believe it is wrong, for you it is wrong because you violated your own conscience. The same is true of what you drink, what you wear, who you date, what you read, what you watch, and where you live. This principle touches every area of life. Some Christians have tender consciences. They are "weak" in the sense that they are so fearful of doing wrong that they live with lots of personal Do's and Don'ts. For them, eating meat offered to idols is a sin.

Paul says food doesn't matter to God. Food is food, meat is meat, corn is corn, and chicken-fried steak is what we will someday eat in heaven. It doesn't matter if you eat that meat offered to idols or not. God doesn't care one way or the other. Here is where knowledge and love work together to provide solid guidance. Although you know it's okay to eat meat offered to idols, you also know others see the matter differently. For them, your meat eating seems like a compromise. It makes them question you, and it tempts them to do something that could hurt them spiritually.

> My brother's walk
> with Christ matters more
> than my Christian liberty.
> Better that I should
> say no when I could
> say yes, than to take a
> chance of hurting
> another believer.

It is possible while doing something harmless that you may become a stumbling block to someone else.

Let's run the clock back two thousand years to the ancient seaport of Corinth in first-century Greece. One day you decide to eat lunch at the local fast-food joint, The Baal Burger Barn. It doesn't matter to you that there are pictures of idols all over the walls or that the meat has been offered to idols. You order a double-bacon Baal-burger with extra cheese and a soft drink. All around you pagans are eating. One of your Christian friends sees you there and is troubled by your actions. He says to himself, "I guess there must be nothing wrong with eating there." But in his heart he believes Baal is a real idol with real power. So he walks in and orders a meal, all the while feeling guilty and sinful. Two bad things have happened: he violated his conscience and therefore sinned, and you acted in an arrogant manner without consideration of his feelings.

We don't live alone, but in a community of believers. What one person does impacts all the rest. It matters what we do and where we do it, even when the activity itself is not sinful.

❧

Can we eat meat offered to idols or not? Yes, of course we can. But the bigger question is not can we? but should we? Paul's answer is, it depends. If you know of other Christians who struggle in this area and who look to you for inspiration, the answer is no. If you care about your brother or sister, you will voluntarily limit your Christian liberty.

I believe Paul's teaching applies mostly to new believers and young Christians. We must be careful not to hurt the newest plants in the Lord's garden. Our careless behavior may cause them to wither and die.

Our behavior has consequences we may not see at first. Our casual attitude may hurt those who watch us day by day. Our loose language, our tendency to answer in a cutting manner, our casual attitude toward the things of the world may influence another believer to compromise his convictions. We must never let that happen. Too much is at stake. My brother's walk with Christ matters more than my Christian liberty. Better that I should say no when I could say yes, than to take a chance of hurting another believer.

❧

Behind this teaching stands the truth of the body of Christ. If we believe that we are all part of Christ's body, we will take extra care lest we should hurt another part of the body.

❧

Do we believe in Christian liberty? Absolutely! Christ died to set us free from the law. We are no longer bound by the old system with its rules and regulations. But Christian liberty does not mean "anything goes." We are free, not to do what we want but only what God wants. We are free, not to flaunt our liberty but to live in a community of believers where some may not be as strong as we are. Christian liberty must be guarded by Christian love and Christian responsibility. If we love Christ, we will never do anything to needlessly hurt His little ones.

Spirit of God, Make me sensitive to those around me, lest I should needlessly harm another child of God. Give me wisdom to walk without offense to those who watch me every day. Amen

Is it okay for Christians to eat meat offered to idols? In what sense is the answer yes? In what sense is the answer no?

How would you answer a Christian who said, "I can't worry about what other people think. The only person I answer to is God"?

What does the phrase "responsible Christian liberty" suggest to you?

Is There a Servant in the House?

Luke 22 : 27

"*For who is greater, the one who is at the table*

or the one who serves? Is it not the one who is at

the table? But I am among you as one who serves."

Three times I have traveled to Haiti, the poorest country in the Western hemisphere. I'll never forget my first visit. I thought I knew what poverty was, but as soon as I got off the plane, I knew I was in another world. I spent most of my time in Pignon, a town of thirty thousand with ninety percent unemployment, no running water, no newspaper, no TV, no radio, no electricity, no paved roads.

I met Pastor Sidoine Lucien, a native Haitian. He founded the Jerusalem Baptist Church in 1977 with sixty-five people, forty-seven of whom had the last name of Lucien. Today the church attracts more than 1000 each Sunday morning to an open-air sanctuary that in America would seat 250 people. Most weeks the offering is under $100. On a budget of less than

$2000 per year they run the church with six associate pastors, three homes for widows, an elementary school, and an orphanage. They are buying land to build a Christian camp.

The pastor is a good man with a giving heart. While I stayed in his home, I couldn't figure out who was in his family. There were people coming in and out at all hours of the day and night. They would come to bring food, come to get food, or start cooking for a while then leave. Fifteen or twenty kids would come in then leave. Who were they? "They are my family."

Over the years, Pastor Lucien has adopted between thirty and fifty kids. One night I met Wilda, a little girl about eight or nine years old. Even though her father is a witch doctor, he respects Pastor Lucien. He told his daughter to go live with the pastor, because "He will tell you about Jesus so you won't go to hell like me."

The first associate pastor is thirty-five-year-old Pastor Eli. Where did Pastor Eli come from? "I raised him," says Pastor Lucien. "I adopted him as a young boy. I raised him, led him to Christ, taught him the Bible, and he is now my associate pastor. The same is true for four or five other men." That's a unique way to build a church staff.

After I had been in Haiti about a week, I saw people walking barefoot for two and a half hours on dirt roads to come to church services. I saw women come into the house with three or four chickens and make it into a meal for fifty people. I saw them give and give and give. Finally, I had to ask, "How do you do this? What is the secret here?"

"Our church is not like the other churches of Haiti," Pastor Lucien replied. "In the other churches, most of the pastors are dictators. They have never learned anything else. They just say, 'Do this, do that.' Their people have to do it. God showed me years ago a different way. All I do is help the people He sends me. When I help them, God sends me more. He always gives me whatever I need."

Then he gave me, in broken English, the best one-sentence statement of what it means to be a servant that I have ever heard: "When I help some, God helps me." You have heard it said, "God helps those who help themselves." Not true. God helps those who help others.

❧

We don't have a
leadership crisis, we
have a servanthood crisis.
Too many people want
the big office, the title,
the power, the perks, and
the prestige. We don't
have enough people
who are willing to work
behind the scenes.

❧

Frank Warren said it this way, "If you want to be a leader, you're going to end up frustrated in life, because few people want to be led. But if you aim to be a servant, you'll never be disappointed."

We don't have a leadership crisis, we have a servanthood crisis. Too many people want to be first, want to lead the parade, want to be on top of the heap, want the big office, the title, the power, the perks, and the prestige. We don't have enough people who are willing to work behind the scenes. We don't have enough people who want to wash dirty feet. The question is not, where are the leaders? The question is much simpler than that: where are the servants?

Are you looking for leaders? Go find the servants, that's where the leaders are. They are not the big shots sitting at the head table. They are the men and women in the kitchen preparing the meal.

*Heavenly Father,
We thank You that You
have made it simple.
Forgive us for chasing
after the world's definition
of leadership. Lord Jesus,
do whatever it takes to
make me a servant
like You. Amen*

Why is servanthood the essence of good leadership?

*Are there any "dirty feet" around you that need washing?
What are you going to do about it?*

*Think about the servants you have known. Give thanks to
God for their influence on your life.*

Mercy
People

Matthew 5 : 7

"Blessed are the merciful,

for they will be shown mercy."

A thousand years from now, what will historians say of us? In the history of the human race, this will not go down as a merciful generation. There has been too much killing, too much cynicism, too much moral decay. Who would dare walk the downtown streets of a major American city after dark? Who is surprised by news of another corrupt politician? We are the most technologically advanced nation in the world, but it seems to make no difference in the way we treat people.

Jesus died to create a race of merciful men and women. A race of men and women who have received mercy and gladly give it away. A race of men and women who would go into this wounded world and bind up the broken. What an impact those mercy people could make in our generation. No gift is more needed.

There are so many hurting people. Behind almost every door is a story of sorrow and disappointment. Name a human problem. You can find someone in almost any church struggling with it: divorce, abuse, incest, neglect, homosexuality, AIDS, alcohol, suicide, drugs, wayward children, alcoholic parents, abortion, depression. It's all there.

The Bible says there is such a thing as the gift of mercy. People with this gift have a special ability to see the needs of others, their hearts are easily touched, and they instinctively reach out to those who hurt. They lead us and guide us in reaching out to the people we might tend to overlook. They understand the language of the heart, and they can see past a casual smile. Their greatest joy is to lift the burden from someone struggling under a load. They love to work one-on-one, they don't want to be paid, and they aren't looking for publicity. They are God's unsung heroes.

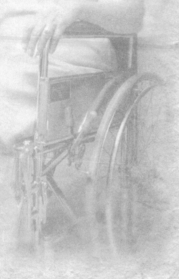

It's easy to see who is on the receiving end of the gift of mercy: the hurting, the helpless, the blind, the deaf, the sick, the infirm, the elderly, the handicapped, the dysfunctional, the shut-ins, the grieving, the imprisoned, the suffering, the weak, all those who are emotionally distraught. But these are the people we tend to overlook because they live on the fringes of life. They don't fit the pattern of being healthy, happy, and all-put-together. It's easy to skip them, to pass on by. But mercy people stop because they see the people the rest of us miss.

I've known a few people like that. What a blessing (and challenge) they are. My secretary in Texas had the gift of mercy. You could see it in her eyes. Gretchen would cry at the drop of a hat, because her heart was so tuned to the needs of others. More than once I came out of my office to find her wiping her eyes as she talked on the phone.

When a father in our congregation suddenly died, Gretchen wept when she gave me the news. Although he was only in his late forties and in apparently good health, he had died of a sudden heart attack. I went over to comfort his wife and their son as best I could, but it wasn't easy; I hardly knew what to say. Merciful Gretchen packed her suitcase and spent the night with the wife. Gretchen's husband had died in an accident some years earlier, so she knew what the wife was going through.

She stayed with Vickie that night and most of the next day. No one told her to do that. She just did it. What a difference it made. That's mercy in action. If it means moving in overnight, you do it. If it means fixing a wheelchair lift, you do it. If it means providing heating pads and black bean soup, you do it. Mercy is seeing a need and moving to meet that need in a compassionate way.

In the famous parable of the Good Samaritan (told in Luke 10:30–37), who passed by on the other side? First a priest, then a Levite. It was the religious people who didn't have time or didn't care or were afraid to get involved. Who stopped to help that poor man? It was a Samaritan, a hated half-breed, a man the priest and Levite despised, who saw the man and took pity on him. It was the Samaritan who bandaged his wounds, who administered the oil and wine, who put him on his donkey, took him to the inn, and paid for his room out of his own pocket.

❧

Mercy is seeing
a need and
moving to meet
that need in a
compassionate way.

❧

"Which of these three do you think was a neighbor to the man who fell into the hands of robbers?" asked Jesus. The lawyer answered, "The one who had mercy on him." Jesus told him, "Go and do likewise" (Luke 10:36–37).

Who is my neighbor? My neighbor is anyone in need who crosses my path whose need I am able to meet. That's simple enough. Mercy is nothing more than meeting the needs of those around me with the resources I have on hand.

Mercy is not an organization or a program. It is people caring enough to get involved. Mercy is nothing more than caring for people the way God does. As Peter Marshall said, "May we put our hearts into our work, that our work may get into our hearts."

Let us go into a world in need . . . and show them mercy . . . show them Jesus . . . show them God's love.

Father,
May I show
the same mercy
to others
that You have
shown to me.
Amen

Recall a time when you were on the receiving end of mercy.
What impact did that experience have on you?

Why is mercy in such short supply?

Think of the mercy people you know. Find a way to say
thanks to one of them this week.

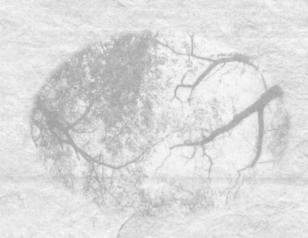

More Than Conquerors

Romans 8 : 35 – 37

Who shall separate us from the love of Christ? Shall trouble or

hardship or persecution or famine or nakedness or danger or sword?

As it is written: "For your sake we face death all day long; we

are considered as sheep to be slaughtered." No, in all these

things we are more than conquerors through him who loved us.

Romans 8:35 lists seven things somebody might think can separate us from the love of God. What about trouble? No. Hardship? No. Persecution? No. What about famine? No. Nakedness? No. Danger? No. Sword? No. All these things could happen to the people of God. You could have persecution. You could have trouble. You could someday face the sword. You could someday be naked. You could someday be living in famine. You could someday be persecuted for your faith.

The next verse reminds us the world considers us as sheep to be slaughtered. That, too, may happen. Martyrdom is a terrible reality for some of God's people scattered around the world.

Who can separate us from the love of God? The answer is still *no one*. Christ is not fickle. Those He loves, He loves forever. Those He saves, He saves forever. Sometimes Christians worry about whether their faith is strong enough to take them to heaven. They get scared and say, "I'm hanging on to Jesus. But what if I lose my grip?"

That can happen. If your salvation depends upon your hanging on to Jesus, you could be in trouble. It's like a little child who is hanging on to his father's finger. The child is doing well until he begins to slip. As he falls, the child accidentally lets go of the father's finger. But when the father reaches down, he doesn't grab a finger. He grabs a hand. When the father grabs the child's hand, it's not the child hanging on to the father. It's the father hanging on to the child.

You are not going to heaven because you are hanging on to Jesus. You're going to heaven because Jesus is holding on to you.

Even so, you are not going to heaven because you

are hanging on to Jesus. You're going to heaven because Jesus is holding on to you.

For half a century Ruth Hall was a member of the church I pastor. After years of good health she contracted a disease that slowly took her life. When I visited her before she died, I found her spunky and cheerful, smiling despite enormous physical difficulty. "The doctors have said a month or two or three, and that's it," she told me. "I'm praying that the Lord would heal me, but it doesn't matter. If I am healed, I'll live longer, but if I die, I'm going to heaven. It's going to be okay, either way." That's what Paul is talking about. Though we face death, we are more than conquerors.

Jesus still loves you, though you may be going through a hard time. Jesus still loves you, though you may be out of money. Jesus still loves you, though your body may be wasting away on the outside. Jesus still loves you, though you may be persecuted for your faith. Jesus still loves you, though your marriage may be falling apart. Jesus still loves you, though the world may be against you. Jesus still loves you, though you may feel like the lamb being led to the slaughter.

Trouble can take many things away from the people of God. It can take our happiness, our prosperity, our health, our friends. But trouble cannot take away the love of God that is in Christ Jesus. That is why we can overwhelmingly conquer even in the worst life has to offer.

Romans 8:37 says we are more than conquerors. That's five words in English. In Greek it's only one word. But it means super-conquerors. We are super-conquerors through

Jesus Christ who loved us. And we are more than super-conquerors.

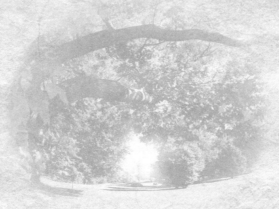

How can that be? Consider this. The only things trouble can take away from you are the things that don't ultimately matter. The things that matter, trouble can't touch. Your life with Jesus Christ, the forgiveness of your sins, your justification with God, the inner joy of the Holy Spirit—the devil himself can't steal that away. That makes you more than a super-conqueror.

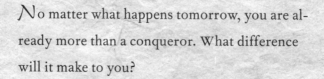

No matter what happens tomorrow, you are already more than a conqueror. What difference will it make to you?

Lord Jesus,
I love You with all
my heart. You alone
are my hope in this
life and in the life to
come. Grant me true
faith to run the race
to the end for Your
glory. Amen

Read Romans 8:31–39 aloud. Circle every statement that adds to your security as a child of God.

How can a person be more than a conqueror in the face of trouble, hardship, or persecution? Who have you known who lived like this?

What habits help you be more than a conqueror, despite daily trials?

Nothing Can Separate Us

Romans 8:38-39

For I am convinced that neither death nor life, neither

angels nor demons, neither the present nor the future,

nor any powers, neither height nor depth, nor anything

else in all creation, will be able to separate us from

the love of God that is in Christ Jesus our Lord.

I t is no exaggeration to say we are standing on holy ground. Like Moses of old, we should take off our shoes as we approach the words of this famous text. Every word is precious, but I especially call your attention to the first four words: *"For I am convinced."* They speak of Paul's personal conviction. Here the heart of the great apostle is fully revealed.

There are times in life when what is needed is logical argument and other times when what is needed is personal testimony. Both are necessary. There are times when someone will say to us, "I have heard everything you have said. Now just tell me what Jesus Christ means to you." At that point, argument ends and testimony begins.

Wise is the Christian who knows the difference. Sometimes we argue, sometimes we testify, sometimes we do both. In Romans 8 Paul does both. Mostly he argues. In fact, this chapter is almost entirely argumentation until he reaches the last few verses. At that point, having exhausted his arguments, having logically clinched his point, he sets out his personal testimony. "Paul, do you believe what you are saying? We hear your words. Now let us see your heart."

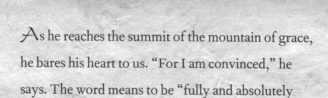

As he reaches the summit of the mountain of grace, he bares his heart to us. "For I am convinced," he says. The word means to be "fully and absolutely persuaded on the basis of evidence that cannot be denied." In the Greek he uses a perfect tense. It means something like "I used to believe this and I still believe it today." When Paul says he is persuaded, he speaks as a man who has staked his life upon certain unchanging realities: "I was sure about this yesterday. I am totally convinced today. By the grace of God I will be even more certain tomorrow."

These verses may seem complicated. But Paul is saying one thing and one thing only: "I am convinced that nothing can separate us from the love of God." Everything else is additional amplification. The word "separate" means "to violently tear from, to completely divide." Paul says nothing that can happen to us can completely separate us from the love of God.

There is one qualifier we need to notice—"Nothing can separate us." Who is the "us" of verse 39? Those who are "in Christ Jesus." This promise applies to believers and only to believers. It is not a general statement describing everyone in the world. Only those who know Jesus Christ through saving faith may claim this promise; we will never be separated from the love of God.

Then the question comes, "Paul, are you sure about that? You speak so confidently. Isn't there something, somewhere that could possibly, somehow, someway separate us from the love of God?" Good question. To answer it Paul sets forth ten possible things that might separate us from the love of God. These ten possibilities are set forth in four sets of two each, with two items set off by themselves. Taken together, they encompass everything in the universe. He includes every imaginable realm of existence.

- life or death
- angels or demons
- the present or the future
- all spiritual forces
- height or depth
- anything in all creation

There is nothing that is or ever could be—nothing you could dream or imagine—that could separate a believer in Jesus from God's eternal love.

Sometimes people say, "But what if I want to separate myself from God's love? What if I take myself out of God's love? What if I decide I don't want to be saved any longer? What if I decide that I want to be un-saved, un-born again, un-justified? Can I take myself away from God's love?" Good question. Look again at the text. It says, "Any created thing." Are you a created being of God? The answer is yes. Then even you can't separate yourself from God's love. Those God loves, He loves forever. Those God saves, He saves forever. Those God justifies, He justifies forever. If by faith you have come to Jesus Christ for salvation, He will never cast you out (John 6:37), and He will never allow you to cast yourself out.

Paul said, "I am convinced; I am persuaded; I am sure; I am certain these things are true. Nothing in all the universe can separate the people of God from the love of God." What are the grounds of his persuasion? Not sentimental optimism or happy-ever-after-ism. It is based squarely on the fact that God loves us and proved His love in the death of His Son. After

Calvary, no one can ever doubt the greatness of God's love. The cross proves the love of God.

~

Paul said, "I am convinced; I am persuaded; I am sure nothing in all the universe can separate the people of God from the love of God." What are the grounds of his persuasion? It is based squarely on the fact that God loves us and proved His love in the death of His Son.

~

Are you persuaded? Paul was convinced. I am convinced. Are you convinced? Can you truly say, "I no longer have any doubts. I know God will keep me safe to the end"? If you are not certain, it is because you are looking to yourself and not to the Lord.

Take a good look at Jesus, and you will be convinced.

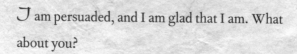

I am persuaded, and I am glad that I am. What about you?

Father, Thank You for love that will not let me go. Thank You for holding on to me even when I let go of You. Thank You for a salvation that will take me all the way to heaven. Amen

If you died tonight, do you know for certain you would go to heaven? Why or why not?

As it applies to your relationship with God, how would you complete this sentence: "For I am convinced that _____."

How can you share the love of God with someone else today?

Love That Lasts Forever

My favorite verse about love is 1 Corinthians 13:7, which says love "always protects, always trusts, always hopes, always perseveres."

Many years ago a young man came to ask my advice about a decision. He was enrolled in a graduate program and wondered whether he should continue. My advice was simple: "Is this what you want to do with your life? If it is, then stay with the program. If not, get out." The young man decided to stay in the program and within a year, earned his degree. That decision led him to make a major career change. For several years he did well in his new job until he suddenly (and publicly) lost his job.

At the lowest point I talked to his wife. With tears in her eyes, she protested her husband's innocence. "I know him. He would never do what they are accusing him of." From that low point the young couple began to rebuild their lives. Eventually the young man decided to return to school to earn another advanced degree, a decision that required him to hold down a full-time job and a part-time job, while he was a full-time student.

As his birthday approached one year, the wife was casting around for a way to surprise her husband. Then she remembered—he had always wanted to go sky diving. Why not now? So for his birthday, she gave him an afternoon of sky diving lessons and three hours to jump out of airplanes. He jumped and survived. With a smile he went back to his studies and earned a degree from one of the top universities in America.

He owed it all to three things: thousands of hours of hard work, a refusal to be turned aside by adversity, and most of all, to a wife who never stopped believing in him. She gave him the benefit of the doubt, she sacrificed for him, she laughed when he jumped out of the plane, she held her breath until the parachute opened, and she cheered when he landed safely.

Love believes the best is possible. Love gives the benefit of the doubt. Love takes people at their highest and best—not at their lowest and worst.

❧

I never tire of repeating this simple truth: People become what you believe them to be. They either live up to or down to your expectations. If you treat a man as trustworthy, he will strive to prove himself worthy of your trust. If you tell a child, "Take a big swing. You can hit that ball," he'll go to the plate and get a hit. If you treat your wife as the most beautiful woman in the world, she will grow in beauty and be transformed before your eyes.

❧

Love sees what might be and acts as if it already is.

Faith moves mountains, and hope never gives up, but love outlasts them all. "And now these three remain: faith, hope and love. But the greatest of these is love" (1 Corinthians 13:13).

Notes

1. *Today in the Word*, Moody Bible Institute, Chicago, 19 June 1992.

About the Author

RAY PRITCHARD (Th.M., Dallas Theological Seminary; D.Min., Talbot School of Theology) is senior pastor of Calvary Memorial Church, Oak Park, Illinois, where he lives with his wife and their three children. He is the author of *Keep Believing; Green Pastures, Quiet Waters; The ABCs of Wisdom; Something New Under the Sun;* and *An Anchor for the Soul.*

Moody Press, a ministry of Moody Bible Institute, is designed for education, evangelization, and edification. If we may assist you in knowing more about Christ and the Christian life, please write us without obligation: Moody Press, c/o MLM, Chicago, Illinois 60610.